Completion of Life

What are you willing to do to find heaven

Nicole Leigh

To my children,

When one went home before me, I had to find a way to be in two places at once. Heaven is a state of mind and level of consciousness. We are a soul made of energy. To reach heaven the wounds of the soul need to be healed. Love is the only answer. It is a love that is beyond space and time. God is love, the road less traveled.

The Hospice Heart

The hospice heart is one that is rare

The space to practice tender, love, and care

Compassion and strength become your superpowers along with a bit of grace

A whole new world with a more beautiful pace

It's not for everyone; yet we all see the end

How beautiful to witness with a nurse who is also a friend

Hugs become a part of life you hold dearly every day

They share the meaning of love when at a loss for words to say

Stop, listen, take a look around

Nothing is as it seems; everyone taking without a sound

Can you feel me mom, I'm still here

 If you focus on the love and have no fear

Trust in my presence for it was always unseen

This is all just a frequency, kind of like a dream

I live in the space that brought me home in your heart

The most beautiful creation and my greatest work of art

Night and day keep passing, yet time doesn't move

Like being stuck in a vacuum with nothing to lose

Pride blocking a meaningful connection

Always guarding a heart and stopping affection

Forgiveness can only carry us so far

Like wishing upon a falling star

The magic only happens when we dig in

When we hold each other accountable as time doesn't end

Bible

In blink of an eye, in the silence of a yawn

Everything precious, lost in the dark while they sing a song

Take a look around, see the ones I love

Care about your neighbor, when push comes to shove

When the only self you see is you

The message is lost sitting in a pew

Reciting verses of days gone by

Singing praises of saints without connection on high

The book of magic available at your fingertip

How do we share the love if we can't receive it

It starts in the heart, the place I am found

The highest vibration, the light that has no sound

It is all but a feeling, when you walk in their shoes

Where do they need love, I have nothing to lose

You took the pen and wrote my story

Stealing from my life all of Gods glory

All that was lost was returned and more

Never again, I am not the same as before

You taught me live in the most heinous way

What not to do and what not to say

The years of turmoil came to an end

When I looked in the mirror and found my best friend

I pray you can find the same friend I found

In the silence of loss, the truth has sound

Say my name and know that I live on

The name you gave me became my song

Morals and values are where it's at

They can steal your show or make you a class act

Character counts to the one above

Healing broken hearts with the meaning of love

How do you treat me, it shows who you are

Are you a good student, or did you not get that far

Feel your feelings but do not project your pain

You have everything to lose, and everything to gain

When we look in the mirror and see who we are

Make sure you life has earned a gold star

God

The land, the sea, the air I gave to you

To hold sacred and take care, what is it going to take to follow through

You have the ability to heal, I buried it deep in your heart

Put down the ammunition and take care of my art

Words can cause harm or be like honey

Soothing the broken or just taking their money

How can we all come to an agreement

It is all about love and the way we teach it

To hold hands in prayer for all, especially the needy

To put down our façade and stop being greedy

I created the heavens for my children to receive it

The light from above, by biggest achievement

When we dig deep and heal the score

Life is not a competition and should not be a chore

Laughter and joy are music to the heavens

The work was done by day number seven

How do we stop the pain we are in

How to love one another and be a good friend

It starts with the basics of human desire

The animal level that fuels the fire

How do we see everyone as human

We take off the mask and we have our conclusion

My neighbor is no better than me

We are more than a body, the heart is the key

When the feeling of love reverberates through the verses

We heal the damage of ancestral curses

I am you, and you are me

Take the time to repair history

This world is all make believe if you teach your children not to give and only to receive

The veil is casts upon your eyes

Pray it is lifted; it is all a disguise

When we all become one in the eyes of the lord

We will have taken the message and strummed the right chord

If you can't figure it out here; How do you think we will get along there

The labels are gone and there is only love to share

The vessel that housed your essence is gone

To join the choir you must sing the right song

Holy, holy, holy is the word they exclaim

Do not tarnish another with your own shame

Transparency is best when you are filled with light

No place to hide, you are always in sight

Your heart should be pure to make the journey home

No rest for the wicked, they will forever roam

The vibration of loves eternal bliss

Brought down to earth as you wish

What will you pray for, will it be words for all

No one is bigger, or better, or small

Each has a gift just waiting to discover

I tucked it inside the heart of a mother

She uses her words to uplift and rejoice

God gave her a gift in the tone of her voice

How sweet the sound of her words with a bit of honey to follow

Sharing a message in a different way that is easier to swallow

The Crowd

Hate, such an awful disease

It buries a soul and steals your peace

We are not the same; if we were wouldn't the world be a bore

Judging my differences is like keeping score

The scoreboard unnecessary, as we are supposed to love

The message that keeps playing from heaven above

What thoughts do you own, are they even original

You have a unique voice, you are your own individual

If we follow the crowd we may end in the wrong place

Our heart is our home; our holy, sacred space

My cup runneth over with abundance to share

This voice in my heart that tells me to care

Teaching love is lost form of art

It starts in heaven and comes from the heart

Creator

I lifted you up when you were broken

Showing you love when not a friend had spoken

You found this soft, warm place in my heart

How could I know you would play a big part

How could I know I would find what I was seeking

God is funny that way; a bit intriguing

How could I know my life was like a movie

How could in know so many did abuse me

When the show began it was very distressing

By the end it all became a blessing

Finding the voice I was made to silence

Always complicit to the violence

Never again will I be silent for another

Accountability is something I taught as a mother

If we are to ever have peace, we need people to change

The syllabus works best when in the right range

Every week they sing in the right key

Yet it gets left at the altar, sacrificing a dream

A dream of a savior it bring peace to the world

The key is in your heart, give it a whirl

We all have the ability to change

We just have to relate the right message in the right range

To carry the tune beyond the time under the steeple

To hold hands and pray with the people

We all want to know there is something more

The story was always in our dna, written at the core

We can read a book, yet the comprehension will vary

Most just want proof, something tangible they can carry

The evidence that gets them through their days

Leaving them with a smirk of knowing, experiencing God in this place

We get called angels more often than not by the ones we touch

A calling from above we mind as such

To ease the burdens and make sure you rest in peace

There are seven levels and you hold the key

Sometimes I am sad for being me

Why do I feel the thoughts others never see

Why was I made this way, was it a wish

Or is it a really powerful gift

To step inside a person and feel beneath the surface

To understand love with all its curses

To feel another's sorrow and bring faith for tomorrow

Prayers repeated to keep my cup full of light

As I hold their hands and tell them good night

May peace and love be all your story reads

When you watch your movie of your deeds

Why was I made this way, was it a wish

Or is it a really powerful gift

What qualifies as spiritual intelligence

Do you understand love with all its facets

Do you understand the birth of creation

The sacrifice given for a nation

The sacrifice of an only son

A love so strong you try to protect everyone

A love so powerful it heals a broken heart

The part of creation people are willing to extort

To abuse the will of the creator

Everyone praying for a savior

The work is done when we look in the mirror

Changing our tune from covet to fear

When we have fear of the lord

We turn to the others backside and remove the sword

We understand the heart doesn't work correctly of man who projects his shame

The one who takes and takes and refuses the blame

Medicine labels it a disorder in the DSM V

Their behavior ravaging a soul and stealing a life

Is it a disorder or is it spiritual

When God is used as a license to kill

Do we stand by and say no more

When the one we love is abused at the core

When the teachings are taken wrong

That war becomes our peaceful song

The prayer of one nation under God

I met this God and that love said this is fraud

Humans like a science experiment gone awry

Their hearts broken crying out for love of days gone by

A connection cut short for money and power

Who is really in charge, plant that and let it flower

God did not create this world to destroy it

Creation was created for us to enjoy it

So many lost wandering in the dark

An education lost like a flood without an ark

Who is the teacher and who is the student

Do we need a masters degree to prove it

God sending angels in human form over and over again

No on willing to stop their thoughts and listen to their hymn

Do we keep repeating history

Life is all but a mystery

I couldn't be strong anymore, all I felt was broken

The pain immense, I felt like I was choking

The body only attacks when we feed it poison instead of love

These words should resonate and fit like a glove

Is this what it's like to be a human

To hate one another until it consumes us

To turn the other way and act like we don't know

Just so the wealthy can continue to enjoy their show

Oblivious to the part they play in this world

Singing verses but not really heard

Complicit in stealing quality of life

Pick up the bible and put down the knife

God gave us all the medicine we need

Look around at the forest, at the herbs and the trees

Food is medicine not a chemical composition

We will see healing when we take this position

To say no more to an industry that destroys us

By playing God we don't make the right choices

Go has a specific frequency and key

To repair time and heal the broken if we see

God is Love

Man cannot decipher the word of God alone

The energy must reach in and break up a heart made of stone

The hardness that turns its gaze from another

The one who is willing to watch others suffer

It is not a blessing it is not you

How easily it could be when you wear the others shoe

Saying prayers of gratitude for wealth and forgiveness

Everyone ignoring the part that is within us

We are all the same, just trying to find our home

A hero's journey that can only be alone

To bring light to the evil within

My people were chosen before you even had a vision

To remain faithful to my everlasting work

To make changes so my heart does not hurt

Searching through my files for a friend that hears my voice

We all live a lesson, what lesson is our choice

Do I continue to send messages when they fall on deaf ears

The meaning is lost when a conscious is not clear

Emotional avoidance often confused as peace

Just like a slow and systemic disease

Don't get involved is the tune many sing

The creator is waiting to crown the king

The beauty behold it shines like a diamond

Our precious commodity all but forgotten

What is the brilliance of the light

It shows you where you are supposed to put up a fight

To bring heaven back where it belongs

The world needs peace, please sing the right song

Love one another as I have loved you

It is all I ask not many but a few

Your home is eternal, a place of beauty and grace

Put down the mask and show your real face

You will not be accepted by ones that are fake

What does it matter, there is more at stake

The level of progression of the soul

It should be paramount to everyone's goal

There are seven levels to achieve

Be careful and weary of the one you cleeve

So easily led astray by a wolf in sheep's clothing

To foster an image of peace and knowing

Words are like weapons or art

You decide if you play the right part

What side of history do you see yourself in

Is it the devil or is it a friend

Put down the weapons and sow the spirit with wealth

It is the only way to have proper spiritual health

Imagine making God cry out in pain

Wouldn't your story all but be a shame

In the eyes of the lord we are supposed to be healers

To take history and change the cold into believers

To soften the sharp edges that cut so deep

To teach love to the wolf that pretend to be sheep

The light is beautiful when we are ready to receive it

It teaches us about love and how to believe it

Home

Your name remains a whisper in my heart

The place I so carefully made my work of art

You came into my home and told me it had no value

Your manipulation, rehearsed from your greed, how could you be so shallow

You almost put out the light of an angel, was it worth it to forever roam

Using her time when she was trying to find her way home

Not able the hear her own voice, so she reached out to God for a sign

Tha was the pitfall of her decline

Not trusting in love; never able to see her own shine

The reflection healed many wounds when able to witness the path that was mine

To see all the way others had controlled the story of life

Taking Gods pen claiming you are my wife

Not allowing for the truth to flow

From the fountain of ink you use from below

Breaking free from the chains of ink on my heart

Love is a feeling and became my work of art

I took the pen back from the ones that had no right to abuse me

Placing God in the narrative has been the key

To focus on love and where this heart belongs

To only share my time with who understands my song

Words can be weapons of mass destruction or healing

Add a bit of honey to you heart and swallow the meaning

Compassion not judgment is the key to connection

Close your mouth and open your heart to affection

See the world through eyes from above; the world of creation

Stand back and observe your thoughts and sensations

What are you feeling and how do you not see

You are you and I am me

You have no right to judge or harm another with your energy

Holding God in your heart will be the right remedy

Narcissist

I have met a demon in the shape of a human being

Manipulative, cold hearted, and mean

Me, me, me is the only word they know

Take, take, take until there is no show

Putting their blame and shame on another

I'm sorry I didn't mean to stutter

Caught in a cycle or is it karma

Refusing to see their own drama

How do we heal as a whole

When everyone looks away from the goal

Heaven on earth just like was created

How do we reach that goal if we are all sedated

Blinded by greed, wealth, and power

The seed of God turned bitter and sour

Who will be the one to claim I know God, the mother of earth

Put the blinders down and change the curse

Imagine treating me as if I was the broken one when my cup overflows

Do you even recognize the face in the mirror or is it a pose

Whose child are you when you look in the mirror

The father or mother, or the life lived in fear

How dare you treat me as if I am broken

 I suffered a loss; the meaning unspoken

The loss of a child; the ugly shoes club

Wanna trade places and feel the love

The answer was written in a book long ago

Life had to change and some had to be let go

To raise awareness to a place called heaven

Please pay attention to the number 7

The light at the end of the week

Burns bright at the top of a mountain peak

Maslow shook hands with the bible on the way to the top

Providing a space of healing and love in a tune I can't stop

How dare you treat me as if I was broken

That's how the light gets in and Gods words are spoken

The softer the berry, the sweeter the juice

When honey flows from the rock if you so choose

The land of milk and honey will be all but a fantasy

Put down the blinders and take a look around for me

I worked for free for half my life

Always a slave and never a wife

What's mine is mine and yours is ours

Stealing your dream and paycheck to keep all the power

Trapped in a darkness no one can see

Please keep telling me what it is to be me

The words never encouraging or a truth be told

How brave you were with the lies they sold

Propaganda at its finest, the mask in the beginning

When time wore it off the message kept sending

Post traumatic stress disorder they say after the abuse

Healing can happen when you shine a light on the excuse

They hurt the ones that are innocent in thought

Who never see through the evil plot

Their minds don't work the same

One for love the other playing a game

Two opposites, one light and one dark

Stop blaming the victim so they can heal their heart

Who taught you how to treat another

Was it your father or your mother

The warmth of the heart, the brilliance of the mind

Compassion and lesson in grace to always be kind

When you love yourself it will irritate some demons

Looking for God for all the wrong reasons

They will tell you that your not valuable in the story of life

Not knowing themselves, always ready with a knife

Do you not see that life is a lesson in love

A vision of beauty from the heavens above

How well do you cling to the creator with judgment in your heart

Your words bringing tears as you tear me apart

Take a walk in someone else's shoes for a day

You may shut your mouth, not your business to say

When everything is dark from day one

God blessed you and gifted you a son

He took him home early, he laid him to rest

When others were hateful he always passed the test

Faithful to love of the mother he knew that always had his back

Never talking sideways or trying to attack

His mothers love always present and came from the heart

The love of creation that was there from the start

The life you live will always show your allegiance

Look in the mirror and show your forgiveness

Forgiveness for the broken song you sing

 A fathers turmoil that started with a ring

Who are you when you look in the mirror

With love the message is clear

You picked up the bottle, just like you were taught

Compassion is lost in your work of heart

The bottle that steals a man's soul

Forever to roam with no place to go

The bottle that changed how you look at the world

Beaten down to their level, your voice never heard

The bottle that stays in the family line

Pray you are different before it's your time

You can put the drink away but your life will not change

Until you face the demons, a difficult exchange

At war with your own self, you project on another

Just remember it all starts with the story of your father

There has to be something more than a human on this earth

Everyone interacting with their ancestral curse

Repeating patterns of days gone by; lost in their story that others have written

Have courage, be brave, you may become smitten

When you look in the mirror all you see is you

The words are but a loss, not even a clue

What you do effects generations

The love trickles down though time among nations

You can't heal a connection with a broken heart

Love is a lost form of art

How beautiful our world could be

Pick up the book, comprehension is key

How do you feel when you take a walk in their shoes

What resonates in your heart like an artists muse

If you were them, how would you feel being treated that way

No place on this earth and words you can't say

The women was created to bring you to love

A beautiful gift sent from heaven above

To cherish, to nurture, to protect, and keep safe

Do all these things and I will show you my grace

The mother is the womb of my creation

A song in her heart if you tune to the station

I put the key in a place highly guarded

Please walk in their shoes and finish what you started

Pick up the book that my messengers have given you

Take a walk in her shoes, you may see the sin in you

We are more than a body, although behold the beauty

Look deeper than that and you will finally see me

Everyone searching for love in all the wrong places

The key is the gold that filled all the broken spaces

When I needed love the most

The devil showed up, he was my host

Nothing made sense to me anymore

I looked in the mirror and couldn't see what I was searching for

Why was this the life I was living

Broken and afraid, yet always giving

I picked myself up and found my way through the dark

I gave myself a go, it was a fresh start

What was important to me and what do I value most

Morals and beliefs that defined the host

I could never look at another and see something less than human

It's not how God works, he uses a lumen

To look in the mirror and see a soul

To make correction, it is the goal

The concept of God and the love are two distinct things

One brings peace, the other brings shame

The book that has too many translations

Please come together in one conversation

Stop using the word of love to suit your ego

The work to be done is right in front of you

A degree in God will get you lost

A life in God will cover the cost

The admission to the greatest show on earth

The gold everyone thinks is in their purse

You can't buy love, boy does the lord know

It's all in the heart, when the wind blows

How well do you know love, a God you can't see

The message from above, please use the right key

God is the refined are of love and penetrates the broken space

Leaving the gold for the human race

He who seeks him shall find the key to the dark

The subconscious mind, such an interesting start

What was your intention with me

I was blind but now I see

How long did you think it would last

Before God took off your mask

I blamed myself for being naïve

Always giving, never to receive

The monster inside you finally made it's appearance

When love was needed most, you were on clearance

Nothing to offer, only to take

Get some integrity for goodness sake

The heart carries it's weight in gold

You thought it was cheap, but you got sold

Don't undervalue love that is real

You won't be left to beg, borrow, and steal

Look in the mirror and see your own face

What do you contribute to the human race

Next time you think to see just a body

Stabilize your foundation for it is shoddy

How dare you treat me as if I was broken

I got left to the wolves in sheep's clothing

The takers, the users, the alcoholic abusers; the darkest space a human can live in

No connection to the meaning of life within

How dare you teat me as if I was broken

I was the one surrounded by wolves in sheep's clothing

Always the one to make sure others were cared for

Setting the bar way below the score

The light at the end of the tunnel is there if we seek it

The love of heaven it's not for the weak

To live the story of love that God wrote for my life

I had to take the knives out of my back and put up a fight

Saying no more to the takers, the users, and alcoholic abusers

No more to a life of darkness and shame for their behaviors

You will not reach the next level with nothing inside

Put down the bottle and set aside your pride

The shame is going to come and the memories will appear

God will be but a whisper when the darkness starts to clear

The whisper of truth will eventually roar like a lion

You find yourself small and, on the floor, crying

How dare you wear a mask to save face

When will you grow up, I gave you the place

The broken part that needs fixing is the heart

Pick up your bible and make a start

You will finally see you as God replays your story

Mark my words just as surely

Before you pass to the next level you get to see you through Gods eyes

Please don't let the heat be a surprise

I didn't have time to be hurt

So I took my education and got to work

Where is this God everyone talks about

Where did he take my son, that's a whole lot of clout

Where is heaven if it is real

Would I ever believe it if I couldn't feel

God is a verb, an actions best potential

The meaning of love, it is essential

To understand heaven I had to follow my heart

My life became a beautiful work of art

The light is real and radiant and beautiful

Come take a peek behind the scenes of the show

Everyone put down their masks and set aside the character they are playing

The essence of a soul is transparent without saying

Their actions will always speak louder than words

It is how the energy works when you understand the verse

How much destruction did you do in your life to others

Would you allow you to be a friend of another

Put down the mask when you look in the mirror

It's levels of consciousness, have no fear

What makes me your child; is it only what you see

Remember the feeling; that's where I'll be

In the depths of the darkness; I am waiting for you with a light

To take you to where I am, so put up a fight

A mother's love knows no bounds

They keep saying I'm gone; please don't give up, I can hear your sound

I hear your heartbeat beating in mine; it is quite the song

This is where I have resided oh so long

The space in your heart that holds me to you

Please do the work and reach heaven, here is the clue

You understand love and the blessings it brings

Hear my voice still; it has a nice ring

I am always with you; but I want you to come home and feel me

This place is heaven; no body to see

My brain spun like a top and everything unraveled

The meaning of life is love, the road less traveled

Taking me to a higher awareness the puzzle no longer a do it yourself project

To see more than a body, we are not an object

Perspective is always the key

Take one look in the mirror and you are looking at me

To go against the masses is the beaten path

1+1=2, you do the math

Be fearless in your faith, God heals a broken heart

Love wins in the end if everyone plays the right part

Heart

I found the pieces in all the broken parts of my story

It is ok little girl you can come out now, you don't have to worry

Shattered dreams, a soul lost in the dark

Than a friend came along and said, hey you are good at art

I don't have a mother or father, yet I have a heart of gold

Something that cannot be bought and cannot be sold

The lowest bidder will lose every time

I learned my worth with every rhyme

You are the messiah if you so choose

Embodiment of Gods love for all the ewes

God decided that Adam needed a mate

Creating his equal and perfect date

To be nurtured, protected, and cherished

Like a knight in a horse drawn carriage

Your equal created to bring balance and harmony

Life as one; a singularity

You took something that was not yours to take

Stealing a smile for your own sake

A coaster ride of emotions

Enough tears to fill the oceans

Frozen in time, not able to breathe

The audacity, was it easy to conceive

Heart on my sleeve is where I wear it

Like the Red cross, first aid and I share it

If lost and found, please return with urgency

It is my in case of emergency

When I took a step back and looked around

Nothing was as it seemed, no love to be found

I kept stepping back further to see a bigger view

Is everyone insane, not even a clue

Caught up in a culture of abuse

Spun from the web of a recluse

Healing only available if we change how we teach love

No one seems to understand the message from heaven above

Bandages can't heal a broken soul

There is only one answer, God said give me a go

When is sat with my feelings and listened to my heart

I had to make a change, your love tore me apart

I had to walk away and find my home

I didn't belong in the story I was shown

Ripping me to shreds and pounding me to dust

It wasn't my time yet God said, keep living it's a must

How I asked God do I heal this wound your chosen one created

It left me sore, confused, and jaded

In the most intimate way my heart was hurting

Is that the love you felt was deserving

I turned to the book of your childhood hoping for some answers

The light was beautiful, you are a cancer

You weren't a very good student of your Rabbi or your mother

Who do you take after, is it your father

They paid for a good education in hopes to build your foundation

The gold poured into to you since you were born

How could you throw that away when your heart was torn

The book of life is the most fulfilling meal

Save your soul a few bucks and get a good deal

When I studied the education of your foundation

I found myself in the pages, my frequency was on the right station

I understood love and God was pleased

Helping the homeless, the sick, and the diseased

You helped yourself to my sacred space

Not a single thought about the shame you would face

When God took me home the love was absolute bliss

Like heaven on earth and sealed with a kiss

Breathing life into my vessel and the story of creation unraveled

I can see why so many take a road highly traveled

The road less traveled is not an easy path to walk

It is the strongest foundation, the core building block

God told me I had to go back and share what I know

This is not a game, life has meaning, give it a go

You can only fake a vibe for a limited time

The mask well-worn will fall off by design

When the creator asks have you loved like I have loved you

Don't be naked and say I haven't got a clue

What love did you give and what message did you share

I placed people in your life for you to care

It wasn't about you; the whole message is to care for others

Don't do unto me what you do not wish to discover

You either face God here or you will struggle when it is your time

Your life a series of events that replay on your dime

How did you love others, did you even love yourself

Please figure it out before it is your time and get some help

There is a book of wisdom buried deep inside you

Take some time off and listen to the tune

The spark of God placed in your heart

To create heaven on earth, not a world torn apart

Everyone is fighting a battle unseen

Trying to live a life and fulfill a dream

Childhood dreams all but a fantasy

Everyone competing to be seen

Did you forget that I was a friend

The one that showed up and stayed till the end

God protects the broken and keeps them close

Please make the right decision, so you don't remain a ghost

I always thought that if someone said I love you that was the meaning

Ignoring all the ways I was abused while I kept cleaning

Never knowing what healthy boundaries were

That I was allowed to be seen and heard

That I wasn't a slave to others poor behavior

That I had free will and it was my savior

I took a walk away from the crowd

The music more beautiful when I couldn't feel their sound

Layers upon layers of reparations needed were felt

The work began with love and playing the card I had been dealt

Taking back all the broken pieces of my story

Gods love healing a broken heart with glory

Look at how beautiful you are, do you see

You are looking at who I created, you are looking at me

Caring for the broken and needy your whole life

Always under the guise that you were a wife

Never married in Gods name

Only a legal arrangement, it is not the same

Never cherished or loved the way God intended

Always a nurse surrounded by those that need mended

Their hearts not good, their minds not pure

Take a look at the future, do you fear what I fear

Not willing to be another toy in your game of life

I always wanted to be a mom and a wife

Always having to wear a behavioral health nursing cap is exhausting

I would like my home to be filled with patients, it cost me

When God sealed my fate with a kiss

Heaven was so beautiful, I didn't want to miss

I was told go back, that I had work to do

Brush off the dust and take a walk in your shoes

Feel your feelings and listen to your gut

The compass inside is not meant to cut

I know what love is now, it is heaven

It all comes down to the number 7

You will only become who you surround yourself with

Make sure they are role models and have the right pith

To feel the essence of God, you must first know yourself

How do to feel when you access your bookshelf

If your energy is still stuck at the base of your spine

You will never feel love or experience the divine

The root of all problems is the energy is dormant

When you begin the work, God becomes important

Not chasing a high to fulfill a lower need

Allowing you everlasting life if you succeed

We are a soul made from the same substance

The essence of God just waiting to touch us

Everyone chasing the essence in the wrong places

Wearing a mask and hiding their faces

The feeling begins with the point of time when creation began

Lighting up the essence of love of a friend

Messiah is a level of consciousness

You see that is what we are, a thought in the creators subconscious

To bring to light the word of God

Put down the mask and stop this façade

My brain and my body could not handle one more trauma

I was family, how did you not see you created drama

A drama free life is my free will

I don't need a friend with a knife and a license to kill

You broke something sacred and my world fell apart

I was left to clean up a broken heart

I am not a dumping ground for your poor choices

Your head is filled with all the wrong noises

The creator all but a whisper you refuse to hear

Like a locust upon an nation; a Gold star mothers fear

How dare you create hell on earth for another

Not even a thought that I am my children's mother

When I took a look around at the devastation

It was hard not to see through the relation

I pray some day you understand gratitude

It doesn't hurt and it isn't rude

Who we are here is who we are there

God doesn't like all the noise, all the drama, and fear

If you cause someone to feel unsafe in their own body

Please correct your soul, it is shoddy

To treat another with such lack and disregard

Your heart is a weapon and it is hard

I was not just an acquaintance, I was family

How dare you not want more for me

A real good friend is the way you tried to spin it

The words hit me in the gut and made me sick

You were my best friend when I needed one most

How devastating it was to feel I had been seeing a ghost

A mirage of a man I thought held me close

Showing up on thanksgiving even to boast

Sitting at your families table and thinking about me

What is wrong with your head, your message stung like a bee

The "real good friend" struggling to breathe after you used your weapon

Are you psychotic, do you need a prescription

Grace shows up in many forms in life

Consider yourself lucky, I put down the knife

When I pulled it out of my back the wound was straight through

My heart left weeping and broke in two

You broke me down to the level of a scared little girl

Please reread your acknowledgment, may give your brain a whirl

You brought me back to a place in life that needed healing

When I was a teen, someone did the same thing without feeling

I closed the door and struggled to not look back

I didn't know you belonged with the ones that attack

Giving you years to figure it out politely

Reaching out with love ever so nicely

You said you hoped someday I could forgive you for the pain

I am not the one to ask, God feels the same

My memoir is my book of life, not really a mystery

What story do you want to read when you go down in history

You said sorry I didn't mean to awaken something I shouldn't have

The funny part is it wasn't your love

God brought me home and replaced your kiss of death

It was my only wish, one last breathe

To have a beautiful life with a family

You hurt a child's heart, a dream, like a simile

Every little girl dreams of being loved like a wife

It is the heart that keeps us alive

When you bury the heart of a woman in your shame

When you meet your maker, who is to blame

Gaslighting a girl to feel less ashamed

Telling her she was nothing, treating her the same

Years of healing needed to feel whole

You had the key to a personal show

Left feeling less than human and deserving

What message is in your heart you keep serving

You have a purpose to fulfill, God had the final word

In the silence the feelings are heard

Frozen in time, how beautiful a space

God is our fountain of youth, our healing grace

Listen to the silence that speaks loudly in your heart

We are supposed to collaborate, a group project, not separate apart

How do you behave when no one is looking

Would you be proud of all your doing

Take a step back and watch your behaviors

The may be learned as a need to survive, there is a savior

Look in the mirror and see my reflection

God only wants us to feel affection

Everyone making life so difficult

Love is not that hard when the meaning is felt

The hero's journey will set you apart from the crowd

Angels are everywhere, we just have to find the sound

How do you speak to others and treat the less fortunate

Not everyone was blessed, they didn't get a choice in it

Born into the family they did not choose

Walking away, there was nothing to lose

Value is something only you can determine

Life has meaning if fed the right sermon

You pulled me close to you in what I thought was love's embrace

How fooled I was, the devil in place

When did the evil plot begin

Was it at the beginning when you called me a friend

I didn't understand I was an easy target

Vulnerable in the world and standing on market

Crying and alone in a big scary place

And than a "friend" said hey you want to take about it and come into my space

How could a man go so wrong in life

Thought he was ready years before for a wife

Sharing your broken heart at the beginning and all your rejection

I walked away feeling like your infection

It took years for me to see it was not my sin

I cherished you and loved you like you were kin

You brought shame on your family by not making amends

I gave you years to prove you were a friend

Your looks and charm all but a seduction

The tongue of a snake, can you see the malfunction

Playing with fire so you could fill your empty cup

A smile on your face, it hurt so much

I thought I knew the man in the mirror in the beginning

Thought he was leading me to ascending

I let you take the lead the whole relationship

My mistake, I owed myself and apology for the slip

Leading me to a very dark place

Where your thoughts and heart hold space

I couldn't be a part of the game you were playing

You broke my heart and I left without saying

The love is beautiful when we get to the top

I didn't need your lesson, I had to make it stop

You kept twisting and turning the words in my mouth

Playing a mind game, your energy still south

I took a break and sat back and listened

The silence was deafening, I had been conditioned

Conditioned to live the world through your eyes

Imagine waking up, what a big surprise

You had control and I didn't even know

I took back my life and became a star of my show

When I got to see the way you live

I saw the circus up close, no idea how to give

Look like a clown to God I know for a fact

Juggling girls like you are a class act

Using my resources and bread crumbing your time

All on someone else's dime

Charming and deceiving

Sorry I didn't have a Costco card so you could keep receiving

Thinking you had me dancing in your palm at the drop of a line

Using my heart and stealing my time

I put an end to your personal show

My life has meaning and you needed to go

You left me feeling worthless and used

Who taught you the way to abuse

I care about your soul and where it will stay

But that is your job to worry about, have a nice day

You were my friend and I didn't know you didn't believe

Love the the way to mt heart, it is the key

You can't expect wife energy and say you are a friend

Mixed messages are all it sends

You came into my home and acted like I was your servant

Devouring my resource like I deserved it

It took me some time to build up the courage to walk away

I cared about you a lot and wanted to stay

You asked me not to leave your life

You treated my like a servant and expected a wife

How could I stay in the box you created for me

I want to love my life too, happiness is key

I do no fit into the space you had open

I play a large part in my show I am hoping

I am not a consolation prize or an after thought

How long did you think you could game this girl until you were caught

You thought you could claim your prize as if it were your own

You hadn't paid the price to claim the show

Taking what was not yours to take by force of deception

Playing the wrong card, feel the reflection

Taking a gamble on a girl who was real

Left you empty inside, you can't even feel

Please be careful next time you whisper those words

You are speaking a language that is a curse

New years day meant something to me

I didn't realize I was invited to be your photographer so you would have a memory to see

Like I wasn't eve a part of the story

Walking away feeling treated sorely

I have never felt so unwelcome inside

You kept asking for my time and stealing my life

Time is all we have, I needed to have value

I play a part too and it is not shallow

I held you in this special place in my heart

Let's have a talk about God, it is a good start

Nothing you did went unnoticed or missed

Always observing and keeping my feelings inside, I couldn't take the risk

If I showed you how soft I was when it came to you

The tears would not stop flowing, what was I to do

I couldn't stay on your roller coaster any longer

You played a card that made you stronger

You man handled my heart like you had no shame

Please tell me again you are not to blame

I couldn't be strong anymore, I was not brave

I needed to perform cpr, I had a heart to save

I did not pursue you, you pursued me

I thought out of love, how foolish I see

All a game to use my heart because I am a giver

I never played on that court, the balls of a taker

I had to block the ball you thought belonged in my court

Take some deep breathes, I had a mess to sort

Playing your game was not in my vocabulary

A game of liars poker, all a show and nothing to see

You had an audience for the show you put on

Your Mexican birthday party, how was the pinata, did you get a taste before it was gone

Falling over and couldn't breathe

The paper thin tissue holding a wreath

The crown of thorns, it hurt, how could you not see

Your view should have told you it was me

I wasn't a part of your equation

Just a body to fill an empty relation

I couldn't speak up, I didn't know what would come next

Too many times treated with disrespect

Breaking through the walls and destroying the foundation

What was the goodness inside you were seeking with conditions

You showed me the love you had

I tried to turn the other cheek, it was bad

I couldn't survive feeling that way, not one more minute of one more day

I had to close the door, I had to walk away

I can't imagine you are so clueless with the view

I didn't have time to explain you to you

Like talking to a wall on a cold dark night

The message was clear, don't put up a fight

You didn't hear me or feel me shut down

Apparently, your party also had a clown

Did you play pin the tail on the donkey too

A child's party game, I wasn't a fool

I couldn't act like I didn't care about me less than you any longer

You asked too much and you were stronger

Crying inside begging God to make the show stop

It was a box office hit in your mind, mine it was a flop

You hurt two mothers that night

Your words hurt our hearts

Tore mine wide open, had to pick up the parts

I stayed silent as long as I could

I know she cares about your soul as she should

I hope she understands the message and assists in correcting your behavior

If you look in the mirror you will see your savior

You are a Jew and I Pray you choose to be a Jewish man

God gave you life and love was the plan

There is a way to fix what you have broken

The inner wisdom of the Torah will bring to life what you have spoken

You told me you didn't care if you were Jewish

Broke my heart for your mom, I bet she was clueless

It is the legacy she works hard to maintain

Left a mark on her door, a visible stain

I cried for both your mother and me

Your weapon of choice hurt, please feel, listen, and see

Meditation is key to healing

Turn off the noise that taught you that feeling

It works like a dream when you surround yourself with peace

Running from yourself will cease

You were born to a Jewish mother, be proud of her

There is so much wisdom, if only the heart could see the cure

You hurt my mind, my body, and my soul

I wasn't will to see how much farther you'd go

One minute we are friends, the next just an acquaintance

Keeping me on my toes, always in the dark and silence

Trying to change the thoughts in my head

We see the world differently, enough said

I wanted love in my life, not an empty friend

What were you thinking when you pushed send

I cried out to God begging for answers

This couldn't be life with all its disasters

I want a love story to leave behind

Not pain and destruction from your kind

A personality disorder is what is the label

The cure is a book, it is not a fable

It clearly states how to treat others

I was a good student, the heart of a mother

I found myself in the pages of your story

Like reading braille, can you feel me, are you sorry

Sifting through the words and reading between the lines

How else should I have interpreted the signs

I was the child who slipped through the crack

An unplanned pregnancy and no father to be had

A teenage mother that never found her heart

Her words like weapons to teat me apart

Costing me my identity for half my life

Never knowing love, it cut like a knife

Brought up in dysfunction and abuse that got worse as years passed

Spent a year in a group home as a teen, free at last

I buried my son and all her children were there

We begged her to get help, with not even a care

If I ever hear her voice again it will be too soon

I grieved the loss of parents, I needed a new tune

I had to find the meaning of my life when my son went home before me

Love is the only way, what God had in store you see

How can you have a beautiful daughter and not love her

That will be her concern when the end of time is before her

I don't owe her peace when it comes her time

She spent over 40 years dimming my shine

When I walked away and closed the door

All I had to do was not call anymore

Days turned into weeks and weeks into years

In silence I heard my own voice and got over my fear

I was deserving and worthy of love

I have been a kind nurse for 20 years, my heart fits like a glove

My superpower is compassion and empathy

I couldn't bare anymore of her apathy

When I looked at her through Gods eyes

I shed a tear for the girl and allowed her to cry

I never know what a mother was

Until I looked in the mirror and felt the love

I never had a father or role model in my life

Verbal abuse was all I knew and I put up a fight

My father chose a career over his first two children

How is it possible to make that decision

Showing up way past the deadline

Never taking time to see if I was fine

I never understood all the damage it caused me

I had to step back so I was able to see

I met the man as an adult again

Treated me like I was the black sheep of the kin

My children cried and felt they weren't loved

As they watched him play with my brother's children, aside they were shoved

You are not allowed to hurt my children

Your absence made me stronger, what was your reason

I would be embarrassed to show up at that stage of the game

Excuses are not love, they are not the same

As I stood staring at my son's body in a casket

I looked over at the family section and they were plastic

The man I met as an adult was not my cup of tea

I needed me more than you, I was more than a nobody

I wish him well when his life comes to an end

He was not a part of mine when I needed a friend

Ashes to ashes, dust to dust

My pain had to end; it was a must

I looked in the mirror and the true reflection

The reason I kept going, I needed protection

I deserved more than the nightmare first husband

Killed my dreams, all but forgotten

A biter and mean drunk

Killing the little girl still in my heart

I always dreamed of a beautiful family, everything I never had

He changed my path in life, stealing my hand

He drank his whole life and ignored his small children

I am not your scapegoat, that was your decision

Our son buried by a man with the same illness

He kept on drinking, didn't stop the abuse

The damage to his brain at this point in life

Brought shame to his soul when our son had died

Treated me like I wasn't his mother

Put down the bottle, the mask uncovered

How damaged can you be to treat me with disrespect

Please seek some help and pay some respect

Do not sit at my sons grave and share your sickness

He was proud of his mom when she found the key to the illness

The bible tells you not to do everything you have done and did to me

Do you care about God, my son is still with me

The pain in his heart when he said he didn't care until I became a Marine

Left me with few words, just sorry, I hope he gets clean

He saw through the mirage of a man full of liquor

His mother always love, while you got sicker

I always dreamed of a beautiful family

I got the best part of you, my kids are the key

I knew I needed healing after my world fell apart

I put Nurse Nicole cap on and performed my art

I took a few steps back and observed and watched behaviors

Removed the subjective part and charted the remainder

I watched myself and fixed what needed mending

I than took a look around to see what else was pending

I observed those around me and charted the facts

I took a look at the chart and took a few more steps back

Patients all around me, how did I never notice

To focused on my life to worry about show biz

Attracting the most broken-hearted men

I always know how to show love when they needed a friend

I decided that my broken heart needed mending

I couldn't handle one more thing before it was ending

I took all my education and used it for its wisdom

Humanities were my favorite electives

Along with religion, psychology, and medicine

I always was fascinated by people and their behaviors

I took a look at my own and knew I needed a savior

The magic started happening when I cleaned up the dusty pages

Took care of myself like I was one of my patients

A light turned on and everything around was brighter

My faith unwavering as I am a survivor

My body started healing all the diagnosis it had been given

All because of emotional pain that it kept receiving

I was given a walk behind the scenes

I am God was the response when I asked what does all of this mean

Heaven was so amazing I didn't want to leave

I knew I had work to do and I pulled up my sleeves

I started repairing a broken life worth living

My best work in my life had always been my art of giving

I got to see my life, present, future, and beginning

As I was taken back when time didn't exist as it was never-ending

The light so bright it caused a lot of discomfort

I had to sort out what I saw before I could disclose it

I see things in the future and paint them before they happen

Now I know how it works as I got the Old Testament in person

Took the pain away from this human condition

Grief is spiritual and not a psychological condition

Everyone is grieving in the form of religion

You were just a puppet, never even real

The lies you sold, they had a certain feel

Dancing on the stage you created

Hoping I would swallow them and remain sedated

I didn't want to be a part of your circus

I want more out of life than family curses

Love never found in all the wrong places

Took off the mask you gave me and showed up as my face

I never took a good look before

Always dancing to someone else's drugstore

How empty can you be to steal someone's love

Do you even have a conscious, times two you shoved

Told me lies and pushed me away

Pulled me close when I didn't want to stay

I always saw more in you than the others

I saw the love between a son and a mother

You made me smile in a soft place in my heart

I know that kind of love, I played the same part

I told you my son would be so happy about you in my life

I had to sort out the ways you expected a wife

I couldn't be more than a friend was the way we decided

Until you needed something more and were uninvited

I deserved a better life than you had concern

You showed me my soul and all the things I yearn

I have a bucket list with only one item

To meet my best friend that God provided

I couldn't be strong or brave any longer

Listening to my heart kept making me stronger

Your words playing in my head like the Olympics

Best award for manipulating, you were very specific

I always thought you loved your family

Until you dishonored your mother, like you did me

You taught me about love and the meaning of life

I deserved more, the key was inside

My heart already on the verge of breaking open

Your weapon of choice, it restored my passion

This beautiful girl buried in time

Found her way out of the dark and is no longer blind

I see through all the words and behaviors

I educated myself and became my savior

You overstayed your welcome in my heart

Your words and actions ripping it apart

I excused you from the table and sent you out of my home

I closed the door, I would rather eat alone

My life has meaning and purpose

You were just a ghost, the depth just surface

My heart still aches from the empty chair

I stared at the door, hoping you would care

Haunted by the love I thought we shared

You were my friend, I thought you cared

I already lived through several versions of you

I had to run before you destroyed me too

I needed a soft place to land

Someone that cared and took my hand

I am not like you, don't you see

I wanted to be all I could be

I crave the stillness of the night

The silence of slumber, no demons to fight

The echoes from others passing by

The sound of love all gone awry

Weapons disarmed as that is the light

Words of love hit air, no time to fight

Meditation is key to fulfilling the dream

Who are you, you are me

I crave the stillness of the night

And God said, let there be light

I never felt loved, I was just being used

Advantage you took of a heart already abused

I didn't know that I deserved me

Someone who understood empathy

I didn't know I could say no

Always scared of the next scene in the show

I put on the mask and played the role you assigned

Hiding the girl who was scared inside

I didn't know how to feel safe

Surrounded by wolves is such a dark place

I didn't know the courage it took

To walk away broken after reading a book

I didn't know you were just like the others

I was sure you were different when I met your mother

I didn't know the game you played

Heart on my sleeve, it needed saved

I didn't know you thought you were more than me

Money the façade only the weak can see

I didn't know how much it would hurt

To be given a taste of heaven on earth

I didn't know

How did you feel asking for my college money to be returned

A degree I have served Veterans with, something I earned

How do you look in the mirror at night

Do you understand God, or has your conscious took flight

You were supposed to protect me from the monsters in life

Instead, you walked away and left a knife

You are not a father or friend of mine

My son saw you through a Marines eyes

The few and the proud, a title he earned

A boy you never knew, you were never concerned

Showed up as an adult and bragged about how well you had lived

Judged me on my struggles, this isn't show biz

Never taking time to get to know me

I am pure love and my heart is the key

My career as a Nurse should be what you reflect on

Oh wait a minute, you never asked a question

I reparented myself and did your job well

Thanks for the lesson, is the shame hell

I needed parents not another patient in my life

I'm sorry you are broken, the healing is inside

I needed role models and advise

Not a mental health patient in disguise

It was not my job to listen to you whine

It is exhausting and not a good time

It was not my job to listen to you brag about your other child

I was one of them, you never cared to find

It was not my job to carry your burdens

I walked away from the family curses

I took control back from the ones who hurt me

Emotional neglect is abuse you see

When I saw you were not capable of love

I shed a tear for the little girl; aside you shoved

When I loved myself like I do my patients

Heaven was real and the love was amazing

Do not come to me asking for forgiveness

I healed your wound, God is in between us

I am not the girl you thought you knew

The love was immense, do you have a clue

You disrespected God when you hurt me

 A hard lesson in love, the soul is the key

I left you clues to connect the dots

I know you are intelligent, use your thoughts

Why would I give you the gifts I did or the book I read

Put them all together and take a spin in your head

Something magical happened to me when I walked home that night

The light so beautiful and magnificently bright

Words are useless when behavior doesn't match

What to believe, I had to take a stance

What do I believe, what you say or what you do

Do you know who you are, here is another clue

I pulled myself out of a darkness unfathomable to most

I wasn't willing to be haunted by a ghost

To bury a child and be told to accept it

Put more dirt on my coffin as I planned to end it

Western medicine has grief and life all wrong

We need to change the tune and sing a new song

I would never have healed the pain of all pain

I would have stayed in my wound and remained the same

Someone kept nudging me to listen to my heart

The place we exist when we are apart

We are a soul made of energy

Our body a vessel only medicine can see

There wasn't a pill or psychological solution

The breath of God gave me life and cleared the confusion

My son is with God, the highest vibration

The frequency of love that cured the condition

Grief is not processed through a medical book

The bible will connect you with the healer it took

Souls all around us in a different dimension

Time and space irrelevant when you make the connection

I needed tangible proof God was real

The world kept telling me not to feel

I needed to know heaven existed

Blind faith was too much resistance

I begged for answers to the pain

Healing only available in Gods name

The grief was changing me, I didn't care about myself

I gave up on love and life that was left

I needed proof to want to stay

The pain I felt would not go away

Surviving minute to minute was not the way

Nothing to look forward to each day

I needed to know where my baby was

Was he gone forever or heaven above

I needed to feel his love

One more hug on the wings of a dove

Two worlds to reveal

One you see, one you feel

God is real and the love immense

The vibration unfathomable and intense

The key to the gate is inside

I didn't want to leave, I wanted to stay, I tried, I tried

God told me no you must go back

I gave you my words with a cheat code hack

How do we ever become whole as a world

When separation is taught to the herd

How do we bring peace to the nations

When babies cry of starvation

How do we bring heaven down to earth

When no one knows the verse

How do we sing in unison

When no one knows the note to begin

How do we love one another

When war kills each other

How do we stop the madness

When all we do is perpetuate sadness

How do we sing Gods praises

When no one puts out the blazes

How do we

I was always searching for my family, never knowing where I belong

Someone that understood my heart and listened to my song

I found my home when God spoke my name

Loving every part of my heart and story the same

God showed me the past and through and adults eyes

The shame was never mine to carry, what a big surprise

I pushed the shame back to where it belonged

To the ones that didn't love and abused me all along

My home was always heaven, why I never fit in

This world an illusion and dirtied by their sin

I took a walk alone and found my own way

To the place I prayed existed as night turned to day

God told me I understood the message and now here is your gift

To see into the future, what a perspective shift

You hijacked my heart when I needed it most

You weren't even real, I was seeing a ghost

You thought you awakened love for you, not me

How arrogant can one person be

I was willing to be your friend until your last days

But I wasn't playing benefits with you, our love was not the same

You taught me to honor my journey

Always watching, listening, and observing

When you disrespected the mother we both care about

God said hey, it's time to go on a walk about

Picking up all the broken pieces that had been missing

A piece of the puzzle that I had been resisting

You taught me that I deserve love the same way I give

A best friend that cherishes me the same way I do him

I thought the world of you and you tore mine apart

It all came out on canvas, it is my work of art

They say the meaning is muse, the part you play in my heart

I never met a man like you, you pushed me to do art

As I kept creating the future was unfolding

I thought I lost my mind as it was molting

What I found was this beautiful girl you see

The one that values love and the bible is the key

Observe your day at its ending

Observe the character you were sending

Was it you or were you wearing a mask

Ask yourself why you even have to ask

Make the corrections and tweak the vibration

Our higher self is a lovely sensation

When surrounded with the right energy

You don't have to fake your life of misery

To not be able to be yourself is exhausting

God mad us unique for a reason, stop holding yourself hostage

The human condition begs to fit in

The condition that pushes us to sin